It belongs to

MW00876857

Class Year

I look like this

Made in the USA
Columbia, SC
01 September 2020

18941327R00057